Life is good.®

simple words from
Jake and Rocket

Life is good.

will donate 100% of its profit
from the sale of this book
to the Life is good Kids Foundation,
established to help children
facing unfair challenges.

Thank you for your purchase.

INTRODUCTION

In 1989 two brothers from Boston started designing tee shirts and hawking them in the streets. They bought a used van and called it "The Enterprise" in hopes of boldly going "where no tee shirt guys have gone before."

For five years Bert and John Jacobs traveled the East Coast selling door to door in college dorms. They collected some good stories but were not very prosperous. They lived on peanut butter & jelly, slept in their van, and showered when they could.

By August of 1994, with a combined sum of $78 in the bank, the brothers considered giving up on the ultimate road trip. And then they created Jake and he showed them the way.

Today, Jake and his trusty dog Rocket have become icons of optimism, and Life is good®—America's little clothing brand that could—is spreading good vibes all over the world.

On the following pages, Jake and Rocket share their very best wit and wisdom, and illustrate that the keys to happiness are all around us.

Optimism can take you anywhere.

Remember, the music is not
in the guitar.

Not all who wander are lost.

Whatever you are,
be a good one.

Youth knows no age.

Good vibes are contagious.

Stick together.

Everything is a
once in a lifetime experience.

Takers may eat well,
but givers sleep well.

Think outside the box.

Don't fight Mother Nature.

Simplify.

Run like a dog.

mix it up.

Do what you like.
Like what you do.

Breathe.

Create your own Happy Hour.

The road to a friend's house
is never long.

Go deep.

Don't knock something.
Build something.

If you don't go, you don't see.

Take your sweet time.

Get out.

Flip out.

Read 'em and reap.

Dream on.

It takes all kinds.

The best things in life are free.

Hold a true friend
with both hands.

Keep growing.

Celebrate.

Five star accommodations
are easy to find.

The pursuit is the reward.

Consider yourself a
lucky dog.

Stay cool.

Sometimes the best conversation
is a game of catch.

Take your love
everywhere you go.

Let it fly.

Color is the daily bread
of the eyes.

Get dirty.

Face the bumps
with a smile.

Stay out all night.

The glass is half full.

In creating, the only
hard part is to begin.

Change your perspective.

Better to light one pumpkin
than curse the darkness.

Who feels it knows it.

Get outta town.

The work will teach you
how to do it.

Write on.

Go with the flow.

Blur the line between
work and play.

The world is your
Entertainment Center.

Get your kicks.

There are always flowers
for those who want to see them.

If you don't live it,
it won't come out your horn.

There's no place like roam.

Style points count.

Sometimes nothing is the
right thing to do.

Laughter has no foreign accent.

The little things in life
are the big things.

Remember where you came from.

We will never know all the good
a simple smile can do.

Meredith Books
1716 Locust Street
Des Moines, Iowa 50309-3023
meredithbooks.com

First Edition. Printed in China.
Library of Congress Control Number: 2007922501
ISBN: 978-0-696-23625-9